If Animals C

MW01277760

Guinea Pigs

CURIOUS
FOX
BOOKS

© 2024 by Curious Fox Books™, an imprint of Fox Chapel Publishing Company, Inc., 903 Square Street, Mount Joy, PA 17552.

If Animals Could Talk: Guinea Pigs is a revision of *What Are They Saying?: Guinea Pigs*, published in 2014 by Purple Toad Publishing, Inc. Reproduction of its contents is strictly prohibited without written permission from the rights holder.

Paperback ISBN 979-8-89094-058-2

Hardback ISBN 979-8-89094-059-9

Library of Congress Control Number: 2023943291

To learn more about the other great books from Fox Chapel Publishing, or to find a retailer near you, call toll-free 800-457-9112 or visit us at *www.FoxChapelPublishing.com*.

We are always looking for talented authors. To submit an idea, please send a brief inquiry to acquisitions@foxchapelpublishing.com.

Fox Chapel Publishing makes every effort to use environmentally friendly paper for printing.

Printed in China

If Animals Could Talk:
Guinea Pigs

Learn Fun Facts About the Things Guinea Pigs Do!

Tamra Orr

I was taking a nap when my buddy walks into the room. I race out to greet him. I'm hungry! I let out some loud squeaks, "WHEEK! WHEEK!" to tell him that I want food. He places down fresh hay and a bowl of water. I chow down. I'm so happy!

Today is a special day because my friend also gives me a piece of broccoli. This is a yummy treat! It tastes sugary to me, and I eat it happily.

Pet Fact:

Guinea pigs stay awake for up to 20 hours a day! They prefer to nap for short periods throughout the day.

Pet Fact:

No one is quite sure how guinea pigs got their name. The animals do not come from New Guinea. They are not a type of pig. They are a type of rodent, like a mouse, rat, or hamster.

Pet Fact:

Some think the name came from how much it once cost to buy the animal in England—one guinea.

My buddy says, "I'll be back soon!" But that makes me sad. I enjoy when we play together. I let out a squeal and wait. The boy knows that when I make that noise, it means to come and play with me. I am letting him know I am lonely.

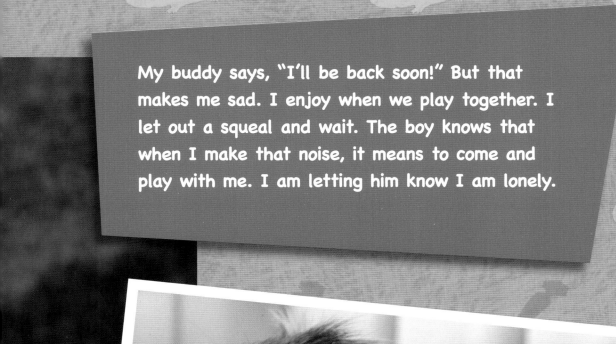

When my buddy does not return right away, I chirp to say I am upset. I have no one to play with while he is away. I am not sure what to do. I hide inside a pile of hay and wood shavings. It is where I feel safe.

Pet Fact:

Guinea pigs are very cautious animals. They hide in hay or tunnels when they are scared or upset. It's important to give these small animals a place where they can hide.

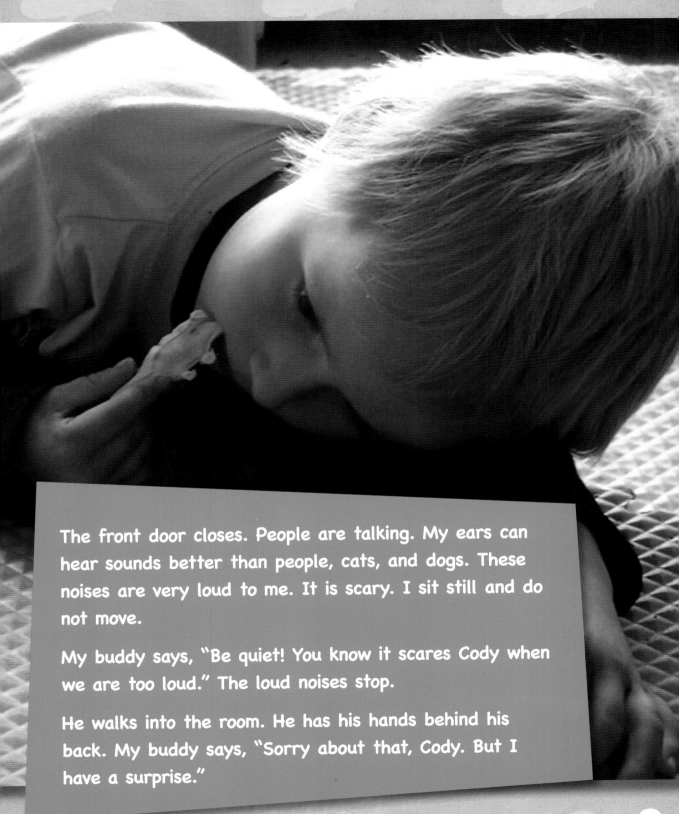

The front door closes. People are talking. My ears can hear sounds better than people, cats, and dogs. These noises are very loud to me. It is scary. I sit still and do not move.

My buddy says, "Be quiet! You know it scares Cody when we are too loud." The loud noises stop.

He walks into the room. He has his hands behind his back. My buddy says, "Sorry about that, Cody. But I have a surprise."

I hear a new noise. What is it? It sounds like the chirp I made when I was upset. Where is it coming from? My buddy smiles at me. He shows me what he has in his hands. It is another guinea pig! I begin to squeal and grunt to say I am happy.

Pet Fact:

Wild guinea pigs live in herds of 10 or more. They are very social! They prefer to live in pairs or with a group of guinea pigs.

Slowly, my friend reaches into my cage and puts the other guinea pig in the corner. "This is Carlos," my buddy says. I can tell the guinea pig is scared. He has puffed up his fur to make himself look bigger and tougher.

I do not mind. I go over to Carlos slowly. I touch my nose to his. He knows what that means—he has a new friend!

In 1961, a guinea pig flew all the way to the moon in a Soviet spacecraft. It flew there along with a dog, some mice, and a few snakes. In 1990, a Chinese spacecraft took a guinea pig, other animals, and plants into space for eight days.

Today, my buddy comes into the room and picks me up. He holds one hand under me. He puts his other hand on top. I coo and purr to show I like it.

He takes me outside and puts me in the play area. It has a fence so other animals cannot get in, and we cannot get out. It has toys like a cardboard box, a grocery bag, a paper cup, and a straw basket.

Pet Fact:

Guinea pigs love to be taken outside so they can graze on fresh grass! These energetic pets will also enjoy the open space to run around and explore.

Hay and grass are foods that guinea pigs need to eat regularly. They will graze on this throughout the day. Vegetables like lettuce, broccoli, and kale provide less nutrients than regular guinea pig food. Veggies are a special treat!

My buddy brings out Carlos. My new friend begins to explore the toys. Then we play. We run through the hole in the box. We chase each other around the cup. We play tug-of-war with the basket. It is so much fun that we begin jumping up and down! Our back legs go up higher than our front ones.

"Look, Mom!" the boy says. "Cody and Carlos are popcorning!"

Our buddy is right. We are doing the guinea pig dance of happiness. We have food, water, toys, a home—and now we each have a guinea pig friend.

Pet Fact:

When you have guinea pigs, it is best to have two boars (males) or two sows (females), rather than one of each because they get along best that way. If you have one boy and one girl, you may also end up with more guinea pigs than you want!

BOOKS

Alderton, David. *How to Look After Your Guinea Pig: A Practical Guide to Caring for Your Pet.* Armadillo, 2012.

Goodbody, Slim. *Slim Goodbody's Inside Guide to Guinea Pigs.* Gareth Stevens, 2008.

Mancini, Julie. *Guinea Pigs (Animal Planet Pet Care Library).* TFH Publications, Inc., 2006.

Pavia, Audrey. *Guinea Pig: Your Happy Healthy Pet.* Howell Book House, 2005.

Rayner, Matthew. *Guinea Pig.* Gareth Stevens, 2008.

WORKS CONSULTED

Birmelin, Immanuel. *Guinea Pigs: A Complete Pet Owner's Manual.* Barron's Educational Series, 2008.

Noah, Hilary. "The Domestic Guinea Pig," Tree of Life. http://tolweb.org/treehouses/?treehouse_id=4713

Pavia, Audrey. *Guinea Pig: Your Happy Healthy Pet.* Howell Book House, 2005.

ON THE INTERNET

BCSPCA: Small Animal Care Series: Guinea Pigs

https://spca.bc.ca/wp-content/uploads/guinea-pig-care-guide.pdf

How to Care for Gerbils, Hamsters, and Guinea Pigs

http://www.hellokids.com/c_20670/read online/reports/animal-reports-for-kids/pet-reports-for-kids/how-to-care-for-gerbi hamsters-and-guinea-pigs

Piggie Care

http://jackiesguineapiggies.com/beforeadoptingaguineapig.html

PHOTO CREDITS: Shutterstock images: Miroslav Hlavko (2–3), Siki_31 (17 inset), vernStudio (18–19 background), Egor Arkhipov (32). Cover and remaining photos:—cc-by-sa-2.0. Every measure has been taken to find all copyright holders of material used in this book. In the event any mistakes or omissions have happened within, attempts to correct them will be made in future editions of the book.